BEYOND THE 9-TO-5: DESIGNING A LIFE YOU DON'T NEED A VACATION FROM

-ABHINAV SINGLA

Introduction: The New Frontier of Work and Life

- Overview of the traditional 9-to-5 work culture and why it's no longer fulfilling for many.
- Benefits of a flexible lifestyle: freedom, autonomy, and alignment with personal values.
- Why this book matters now: the rise of remote work, the gig economy, and the pursuit of purpose.
- A call to action for readers to imagine and pursue their ideal life.

Chapters: Titles and Descriptions

Chapter 1: Redefining Success for a New Era

- Explores how societal definitions of success have shifted from material wealth to holistic well-being.
- Encourages readers to define their personal version of success, blending work, passion, and purpose.
- Discusses the power of intentional living over societal expectations.

Chapter 2: The Myths of Stability and Security

- Debunks the belief that traditional jobs are the safest option.
- Examines risks in corporate careers versus entrepreneurial or flexible paths.
- Shares stories of people who successfully transitioned to more meaningful careers.

Chapter 3: Crafting a Vision for Your Ideal Life

- Guides readers in envisioning their dream life, focusing on work-life integration.
- Discusses the importance of setting clear priorities and goals.
- Introduces vision-boarding as a tool for clarity and motivation.

Chapter 4: Designing Your Work-Life Blueprint

- Breaks down how to create a lifestyle that aligns with personal values and goals.
- Discusses work models like freelancing, remote work, part-time careers, and entrepreneurship.
- Highlights tools and strategies for efficient time and task management.

Chapter 5: Building Multiple Streams of Income

- Explains the importance of diversifying income to create financial stability and freedom.
- Introduces passive income ideas such as investments, online courses, and digital products.
- Provides a roadmap for starting and managing side hustles.

Chapter 6: Mastering the Mindset for Flexibility

- Emphasizes the importance of a growth mindset for embracing change.
- Explores how to overcome fear, self-doubt, and societal pressure.
- Shares techniques for building resilience and adaptability.

Chapter 7: Tools and Tech for Your Flexible Lifestyle

- Lists essential tools and apps for productivity, remote work, and business management.
- Provides tips for using technology to optimize and automate tasks.
- Highlights tools for staying connected and managing work-life boundaries.

Chapter 8: The Art of Balancing Hustle and Harmony

- Discusses how to avoid burnout while pursuing flexibility and financial goals.
- Explores mindfulness, self-care, and maintaining relationships in a non-traditional work setup.
- Shares strategies for setting boundaries and creating time for personal passions.

Subtopics and Subheadings per Chapter

Chapter 1: Redefining Success for a New Era

- *The Old Paradigm of Success*: Money vs. Meaning
- *Holistic Success*: Blending wealth, health, and happiness

- *Your Success Equation*: Defining what matters most to you

Chapter 2: The Myths of Stability and Security

- *The Illusion of Job Stability*: Why no job is truly secure
- *The Real Risks of Playing It Safe*: Missed opportunities and burnout
- *Success Stories*: Ordinary people who took extraordinary leaps

Chapter 3: Crafting a Vision for Your Ideal Life

- *Envisioning Your Dream*: What does a perfect day look like?
- *The Pillars of Your Vision*: Health, wealth, relationships, and growth
- *Tools for Clarity*: Journaling, mind mapping, and vision boards

Chapter 4: Designing Your Work-Life Blueprint

- *Work Models that Work for You*: Freelancing, remote work, and side hustles
- *Creating Your Schedule*: Time-blocking and task prioritization
- *The Role of Experimentation*: Testing and refining your blueprint

Exercises: Practical Tips or Activities for Readers

- **Personal Success Map (Chapter 1)**: Write down what success looks like in five key areas—career, relationships, health, hobbies, and impact.
- **Risk-Reward Analysis (Chapter 2)**: Create a pros-and-cons list of staying in your current job versus pursuing a flexible work path.
- **Vision Board (Chapter 3)**: Cut out or draw images representing your ideal lifestyle. Place it somewhere visible for daily inspiration.
- **Income Ideas Brainstorm (Chapter 5)**: List 10 ways you could generate additional income, starting today.
- **Boundary Checklist (Chapter 8)**: Identify and write down areas where you need to set boundaries in your work-life balance.

Conclusion: Your Journey Toward Freedom

- Recap of key lessons: redefining success, crafting a vision, and embracing flexibility.
- Reassurance that small, consistent steps lead to big transformations.
- A motivational call to action to start today: "Your ideal life isn't a dream—it's a decision."
- Resources for further learning and support (e.g., recommended books, websites, and tools).

CHAPTER 1: REDEFINING SUCCESS FOR A NEW ERA

Introduction: Hook and Chapter Purpose

Imagine working not to escape your life but to enrich it. Success is no longer about slaving away at a 9-to-5 for decades, only to hope for a fulfilling retirement. Instead, it's about creating a life you're excited to live right now.

This chapter is about breaking free from outdated definitions of success—wealth, job titles, and societal expectations—and redefining it on your terms. You'll explore how to align your goals with your values, design a life that integrates work and purpose, and take your first steps toward true fulfillment.

Main Points: Explanation with Examples/Statistics

A. The Old Paradigm of Success

- Success has traditionally been defined as climbing the corporate ladder, earning six-

figure salaries, and acquiring material wealth.
- According to a 2023 Gallup poll, **only 33% of workers feel engaged in their jobs**, suggesting that traditional definitions of success leave many unfulfilled.
- Example: Meet Rahul, a mid-level executive earning a hefty salary but feeling trapped in a job that drains his energy and leaves no time for his passions.

B. A Holistic Definition of Success

- Success today includes emotional well-being, meaningful relationships, financial stability, and personal growth.
- Research by Harvard's Study of Adult Development highlights that **happiness and health stem more from fulfilling relationships and meaningful work than from wealth.**
- Example: Jane, a freelancer who earns less than her corporate counterparts, but spends her days creating art and mentoring aspiring artists, feels more fulfilled than ever.

C. Why It's Time to Redefine Success

- The rise of the gig economy, remote work, and digital opportunities has given us more ways to earn and live.
- Success can now mean creating a lifestyle that aligns with your core values and provides freedom and flexibility.
- Example: Alex, who transitioned from a tech job to running a travel blog, now earns through multiple income streams while exploring the world.

Tips: Practical Strategies for Immediate Use

A. Define Your Success Equation

- Write down what success means to you in five areas: Career, Relationships, Health, Passions, and Impact.
- Example: "In my career, success means having the flexibility to work remotely. In my relationships, it means being present for my family."

B. Conduct a Time Audit

- Track how you spend your time over a week.
- Identify areas misaligned with your definition of success and take steps to adjust.

- Example: If "health" is part of your success equation but you're skipping workouts, reprioritize your schedule.

C. Start Small, Dream Big

- Identify one small step to bring your life closer to your ideal definition of success.
- Example: If success means pursuing creative passions, allocate 30 minutes daily to sketch, write, or design.

Analogies: Metaphors to Simplify Ideas

Success as a Recipe

Success is like cooking your favorite dish. The traditional recipe was heavy on "work" and "money" but lacked seasoning like passion, freedom, and relationships. It's time to rewrite the recipe to suit your taste.

The Garden of Life

Think of success as cultivating a garden. Traditional success focused on growing one massive tree of career achievement, but a thriving garden includes flowers (relationships), fruits (health), and shade (peace of mind).

Summary: Key Takeaways and Next Chapter Preview

- **Key Takeaways**:
    - Traditional definitions of success no longer work for everyone.
    - Success today is about alignment with personal values and holistic well-being.
    - You have the power to redefine success for yourself, starting with small, intentional changes.
- **Next Chapter Preview**:

In the next chapter, we'll tackle the myths of stability in traditional jobs and explore how stepping outside your comfort zone can lead to a more secure and fulfilling life.

Chapter 2: The Myths of Stability and Security

Introduction: Hook and Chapter Purpose

Imagine holding onto a rope that feels sturdy, only to realize it's fraying at the edges. For decades, we've been told that a "stable" job with a steady paycheck is the safest bet for a secure future. But is it really?

This chapter debunks the myths surrounding stability in traditional jobs, explores the hidden risks of playing it safe, and introduces alternative paths to achieving true security—where you're in control.

Main Points: Explanation with Examples/Statistics

A. The Illusion of Job Security

- Traditional jobs are often seen as secure, but layoffs, automation, and corporate restructuring tell a different story.
- In 2023, **over 50% of U.S. workers reported fearing job loss due to economic instability and technological advancements** (Statista).
- Example: Raj, a high-performing manager, was unexpectedly laid off when his company downsized, proving that even top employees aren't immune.

B. The Real Risks of Playing It Safe

- Staying in a job solely for security often leads to stagnation, burnout, and missed opportunities.
- A Deloitte study found that **80% of workers are unhappy in their current roles**, yet many stay out of fear.
- Example: Anita, who remained in a corporate role she disliked, missed out on years of personal growth she later found by starting her consulting business.

C. Stability Redefined: Taking Control of Your Future

- True stability comes from adaptability, diversified income streams, and continuous skill-building.
- Freelancers and entrepreneurs report **higher levels of job satisfaction and control** over their time compared to traditional employees (Upwork survey, 2022).
- Example: Leah, a former teacher, now earns through online courses, tutoring, and educational consulting, enjoying both financial security and flexibility.

Tips: Practical Strategies for Immediate Use

A. Conduct a Risk Assessment

- List the potential risks of staying in your current job versus pursuing a new path.
- Example: Staying may mean financial predictability but limited growth; leaving could bring short-term instability but long-term rewards.

B. Start Building Skills and Side Income

- Identify a skill you can monetize, and dedicate 5-10 hours weekly to developing it.

- Example: Learn graphic design, coding, or digital marketing through online courses.

C. Create a Financial Cushion

- Save 3-6 months' worth of expenses to give yourself a buffer while transitioning.
- Example: Redirect discretionary spending toward an emergency fund or investment account.

D. Network Beyond Your Industry

- Build connections in fields you're interested in exploring. Attend meetups, join online communities, or reconnect with old acquaintances.

Analogies: Metaphors to Simplify Ideas

The Sinking Ship vs. the Lifeboat

A traditional job can feel like a massive ship—steady and imposing—but when it starts sinking, it's hard to steer to safety. Creating your own lifeboat (skills, side hustles, or entrepreneurship) ensures you always have a way forward.

The Safety Net Illusion

Imagine walking a tightrope with a safety net below. The corporate job seems like the net, but if it's torn, you're vulnerable. Building multiple income streams is like weaving a stronger, more reliable net yourself.

Summary: Key Takeaways and Next Chapter Preview

- **Key Takeaways**:
    - Traditional jobs are not as secure as they seem.
    - Relying solely on one job can limit growth and expose you to risks.
    - True stability comes from adaptability, continuous learning, and diversification.
- **Next Chapter Preview**:
In the next chapter, we'll explore how to craft a vision for your ideal life, focusing on aligning your passions, goals, and values to create a fulfilling and sustainable lifestyle.

CHAPTER 3: CRAFTING A VISION FOR YOUR IDEAL LIFE

Introduction: Hook and Chapter Purpose

Close your eyes and imagine your perfect day. Where are you? What are you doing? Who are you with? Crafting a vision for your ideal life is the first step to designing it. Without a clear picture of what you truly want, you risk chasing goals that don't align with your values.

This chapter will guide you through defining your dream life. You'll learn how to connect with your passions, identify what truly matters, and create a roadmap for turning your vision into reality.

Main Points: Explanation with Examples/Statistics

A. The Power of a Clear Vision

- People with a written vision are significantly more likely to achieve their goals.
- A study by Dominican University found that **individuals who wrote down their goals were 42% more likely to achieve them.**
- Example: Priya wanted to live abroad but felt stuck in her 9-to-5. By clearly defining her vision—teaching yoga in Bali—she turned it into a reality within two years.

B. Aligning Your Vision with Your Values

- Your ideal life should reflect what's most important to you—family, creativity, adventure, or contribution.
- Misaligned goals lead to burnout and dissatisfaction, even when achieved.
- Example: Ravi, a software engineer, realized that while his career was lucrative, it didn't align with his value of community service. He transitioned to a nonprofit role, blending purpose and passion.

C. Breaking Down Big Dreams into Achievable Goals

- A lofty vision can feel overwhelming, but breaking it into actionable steps makes it attainable.
- Example: If your vision is to work remotely while traveling, start by researching roles or freelance options that allow for location independence.

Tips: Practical Strategies for Immediate Use

A. Create Your Vision Statement

- Write a paragraph describing your ideal life. Include details about your work, relationships, health, and hobbies.
- Example: "I work 4-5 hours a day from home or a café, spend evenings with my family, and dedicate weekends to painting and hiking."

B. Use the Wheel of Life

- Draw a circle divided into segments: Career, Relationships, Health, Finances, Personal Growth, Fun, and Contribution. Rate your satisfaction in each area from 1 to 10, then identify which areas need improvement.

C. Set SMART Goals for Your Vision

- Break your vision into **Specific, Measurable, Achievable, Relevant, and Time-bound** goals.
- Example: "By the end of this year, I will save $10,000 and enroll in a remote work training program."

D. Visualize Daily

- Spend 5 minutes each morning visualizing your ideal life. Imagine how it feels, looks, and sounds to live it.

Analogies: Metaphors to Simplify Ideas

Your Vision as a GPS

A vision is like entering a destination into your GPS. Without it, you'll wander aimlessly, but with it, you'll navigate toward your goals—even if you take a few detours along the way.

Building a Dream House

Designing your ideal life is like constructing a dream house. First, you need a blueprint (vision), then gather materials (skills and resources), and finally, build it step by step.

Summary: Key Takeaways and Next Chapter Preview

- **Key Takeaways**:
    - A clear vision is the foundation of an intentional life.
    - Aligning your vision with your values ensures fulfillment, not just achievement.
    - Breaking down your dream into actionable steps makes it attainable.
- **Next Chapter Preview**:
In the next chapter, we'll dive into designing your work-life blueprint, where you'll learn how to align your career with your vision and create a sustainable plan for balance and success

CHAPTER 4: DESIGNING YOUR WORK-LIFE BLUEPRINT

Introduction: Hook and Chapter Purpose

What if your work wasn't just a means to pay the bills but an integrated part of a fulfilling life? Designing your work-life blueprint means creating a harmonious plan where your career and personal goals align, complementing rather than competing with each other.

This chapter will guide you in mapping out a sustainable balance that supports your passions, values, and financial needs, while leaving room for personal growth, relationships, and downtime.

Main Points: Explanation with Examples/Statistics

A. The Cost of an Unbalanced Life

- Burnout, strained relationships, and declining health often result from an unbalanced work-life dynamic.
- According to the World Health Organization (WHO), **burnout is a major contributor to poor mental health, with nearly 60% of workers reporting it at least once a year.**
- Example: Akash, a marketing executive, worked 80-hour weeks to climb the corporate ladder but realized too late that he missed milestones with his family.

B. The Benefits of a Work-Life Blueprint

- A well-designed blueprint ensures time for both professional success and personal fulfillment.
- Example: Priya, a freelance graphic designer, structured her schedule to work 4 days a week, dedicating Fridays to personal projects and weekends to family.

- Studies show that **people who intentionally balance work and life are 20% more productive and experience 30% higher** job **satisfaction** (Harvard Business Review).

C. Identifying Your Non-Negotiables

- Define the core elements your work-life blueprint must include, such as family time, health priorities, and creative pursuits.
- Example: Ramesh, a tech entrepreneur, identified that his non-negotiables were 7 hours of sleep, daily exercise, and attending his kids' school events.

Tips: Practical Strategies for Immediate Use

A. Audit Your Current Work-Life Balance

- Track your time over a week and categorize activities into work, personal, and leisure.
- Identify areas where time allocation doesn't align with your priorities.
- Example: Are you spending more hours on email than on personal growth or family?

B. Design Your Ideal Week

- Create a weekly schedule that reflects your ideal work-life integration. Include blocks for work, health, relationships, and hobbies.

- Example: Work from 9 AM to 3 PM, exercise from 4 PM to 5 PM, and spend evenings with loved ones.

C. Set Clear Boundaries

- Establish rules to prevent work from spilling into personal time, such as "no emails after 7 PM" or "weekends are unplugged."

D. Build Flexibility into Your Blueprint

- Leave room for adjustments. Life isn't static, and your blueprint should evolve as circumstances change.

E. Embrace Delegation

- Identify tasks that can be outsourced or delegated at work and home to free up time for priorities.
- Example: Hire a virtual assistant or share household chores with family members.

Analogies: Metaphors to Simplify Ideas

Your Work-Life Blueprint as a Puzzle

Think of your life as a puzzle. Each piece—work, family, health, hobbies—needs to fit together to complete the picture. Neglecting one piece leaves a gap that disrupts the whole.

Building a Bridge

A work-life blueprint is like building a bridge between two shores: one represents your career, and the other your personal life. The stronger the foundation and balance, the more seamlessly you can cross between the two.

Summary: Key Takeaways and Next Chapter Preview

- **Key Takeaways**:
    - Balancing work and life is crucial for long-term health, happiness, and productivity.
    - A work-life blueprint ensures that your professional and personal priorities coexist harmoniously.
    - By auditing your current habits, defining non-negotiables, and creating boundaries, you can achieve sustainable balance.
- **Next Chapter Preview**:
  In the next chapter, we'll discuss building resilience and adaptability to navigate life's inevitable challenges while staying aligned with your vision.

CHAPTER 5: BUILDING MULTIPLE STREAMS OF INCOME

Introduction: Hook and Chapter Purpose

Imagine your financial stability as a stool. Relying on one income stream is like balancing on a single leg—fragile and prone to collapse. But with multiple legs, the stool becomes sturdy and unshakable.

This chapter explores how to diversify your income, why it's crucial for financial freedom, and practical ways to get started. Whether it's passive income, side hustles, or freelance work, building multiple streams ensures you're not reliant on a single source, empowering you to design a life of flexibility and security.

Main Points: Explanation with Examples/Statistics

A. Why Multiple Income Streams Matter

- Relying solely on a single job or business income is risky. Economic shifts, industry disruptions, or job loss can destabilize your finances.
- A 2023 study by Bankrate found that **nearly 44% of Americans now have a side hustle, contributing an average of $483 monthly to their income.**
- Example: Neha, who lost her corporate job during the pandemic, was able to stay afloat thanks to her Etsy store and online tutoring.

B. Types of Income Streams

1. **Active Income**: Requires ongoing work, such as freelancing, consulting, or a part-time job.
    - Example: Arjun uses weekends to offer photography services, adding a steady cash flow alongside his main job.

2. **Passive Income**: Requires initial effort but minimal maintenance, like rental properties, dividend stocks, or e-books.
   - Example: Priya earns royalties from her self-published book, providing her with a monthly income.
3. **Portfolio Income**: Earnings from investments such as stocks, mutual funds, or real estate.
   - Example: Ravi invests in index funds, growing his wealth over time.

C. The Long-Term Benefits

- Diversification reduces financial stress and provides freedom to pursue passions without fear of financial instability.
- Studies show that **individuals with diverse income sources report higher satisfaction and lower anxiety about finances.**

Tips: Practical Strategies for Immediate Use

A. Start Small

- Begin with one additional income stream, such as freelance work or selling a skill online.
- Example: Teach a skill you're good at, like cooking, coding, or graphic design, through platforms like Skillshare or Udemy.

B. Leverage Your Existing Skills

- Identify skills you already have and explore how to monetize them.
- Example: If you're good at writing, start offering content creation or resume-writing services.

C. Research Passive Income Opportunities

- Explore options that fit your interests, such as investing in stocks, creating a digital product, or renting out property.
- Example: Create an e-book or course about a niche topic you're passionate about.

D. Use Online Platforms

- Join platforms like Fiverr, Upwork, or Etsy to market your skills or products.
- Example: Sell handmade crafts or offer virtual assistant services to clients globally.

E. Track and Scale

- Monitor your earnings from each stream, and once stable, consider scaling or adding a new one.
- Example: Scale a side hustle by hiring help or automating processes, freeing you to focus on other streams.

Analogies: Metaphors to Simplify Ideas

The Financial Garden

Think of your income streams as plants in a garden. Relying on one plant (your job) means trouble if it wilts. A diverse garden with flowers, trees, and vegetables ensures something is always blooming.

The River System

A single river (income source) may dry up during a drought, but a system of tributaries (multiple streams) ensures the flow of water (financial stability) even during tough times.

Summary: Key Takeaways and Next Chapter Preview

- **Key Takeaways**:
    - Building multiple streams of income reduces financial risk and increases freedom.
    - There are three main types of income streams: active, passive, and portfolio.
    - Start small, leverage your skills, and explore scalable opportunities.
- **Next Chapter Preview**:
  In the next chapter, we'll focus on mastering time management and

productivity, ensuring you can juggle multiple pursuits without feeling overwhelmed.

CHAPTER 6: MASTERING THE MINDSET FOR FLEXIBILITY

Introduction: Hook and Chapter Purpose

In a world where everything seems to change at lightning speed, flexibility is no longer just a nice-to-have trait—it's essential. Imagine living in a state of constant adaptability, where setbacks are simply stepping stones, and uncertainty becomes an opportunity for growth.

This chapter will teach you how to develop a mindset that thrives on flexibility. You'll learn how to embrace change, handle uncertainty, and turn challenges into catalysts for growth, all while staying aligned with your ultimate vision for a balanced and fulfilling life.

Main Points: Explanation with Examples/Statistics

A. The Power of a Growth Mindset

- People with a growth mindset believe that abilities and intelligence can be developed through dedication and hard work. This mindset fosters a love for learning and resilience, key qualities for adaptability.
- **Stanford psychologist Carol Dweck** found that individuals with a growth mindset are more likely to overcome challenges and achieve their goals.
- Example: Maria, who was laid off from her job, viewed the situation not as a setback, but as an opportunity to launch her freelance career. This mindset shift enabled her to find new ways to earn and adapt quickly to her new circumstances.

B. Overcoming the Fear of Change

- Fear of change is one of the greatest barriers to flexibility. People tend to stick

- with the familiar, even when it no longer serves them.
- According to a **McKinsey report, 60% of employees resist organizational change**, often due to fear of the unknown.
- Example: Tom, a mid-level manager, feared moving to a new role, worried about the learning curve. However, once he embraced the challenge, he found the experience revitalizing and fulfilling.

C. The Importance of Mental Agility

- Mental agility refers to the ability to think quickly and adapt to new situations. In today's fast-paced world, being mentally agile is a crucial skill for flexibility.
- Research shows that **flexible thinkers** are 35% more likely to succeed in rapidly changing environments.
- Example: When faced with a sudden project change, Sita used her problem-solving skills to pivot quickly, presenting a solution that impressed her managers.

Tips: Practical Strategies for Immediate Use

A. Practice Self-Compassion

- Be kind to yourself when things don't go as planned. Flexibility isn't about perfection;

it's about resilience and learning from each experience.
- Example: If you miss a goal or face a setback, forgive yourself and focus on what you can learn from the situation.

B. Adopt a "What's Possible?" Mindset

- Instead of asking, "Why is this happening to me?" try asking, "What's possible now?" This shifts your focus from limitation to opportunity.
- Example: When faced with a sudden change in a work project, think, "What new skills can I develop?" or "How can I make this situation work for me?"

C. Strengthen Your Emotional Flexibility

- Emotions can be strong signals, but they shouldn't dictate your reactions. Work on building emotional flexibility by practicing mindfulness and emotional regulation.
- Example: Before responding to stress, take a deep breath and pause to assess your emotions and reactions.

D. Continuously Learn and Adapt

- The more you expose yourself to new ideas, skills, and experiences, the easier it

becomes to adapt to changing circumstances.
- Example: Make it a habit to learn something new each week—whether it's a new skill for your job or something entirely different, like a new language or hobby.

E. Build a Support Network

- Surround yourself with people who encourage and support your flexibility. They can offer different perspectives and advice when facing new challenges.
- Example: Connect with like-minded individuals through networking groups, online forums, or mentorships.

Analogies: Metaphors to Simplify Ideas

The Bamboo Tree

Flexibility is like a bamboo tree. When strong winds blow, the bamboo bends but doesn't break. It adapts to the wind's force without losing its integrity. Similarly, a flexible mindset helps you navigate life's storms without losing your core strength.

A Dance with Change

Imagine life as a dance, where each step requires coordination and responsiveness to your partner.

When your partner (life's circumstances) changes direction, instead of resisting, you flow with it, adjusting your steps and rhythm to stay in harmony.

Summary: Key Takeaways and Next Chapter Preview

- **Key Takeaways**:
    - A growth mindset enables flexibility and resilience, making it easier to embrace change.
    - Overcoming the fear of change and strengthening mental agility are essential for navigating life's uncertainties.
    - Practicing self-compassion, staying curious, and building emotional flexibility will help you thrive in an ever-changing world.
- **Next Chapter Preview**:
  In the next chapter, we'll explore how to cultivate the habits and routines that fuel your productivity while maintaining a balanced, fulfilling life.

CHAPTER 7: TOOLS AND TECH FOR YOUR FLEXIBLE LIFESTYLE

Introduction: Hook and Chapter Purpose

Picture this: You're traveling the world, managing your business from a cozy café in Paris, and responding to emails from the beach in Bali—all with just your smartphone and laptop. The right tools and technology make it possible to live a flexible life without missing a beat.

In this chapter, we'll explore the tools, apps, and technologies that empower you to work, stay organized, and maintain balance, no matter where you are. You'll learn how to use tech to support your flexible lifestyle and optimize both work and leisure.

Main Points: Explanation with Examples/Statistics

A. The Rise of Remote Work Tools

- As remote work and freelancing become increasingly mainstream, the technology to support these lifestyles has exploded. Over **30% of workers** worldwide now work remotely at least part-time, according to a **Gallup report**. This shift has sparked the demand for tools that enable collaboration, communication, and project management from anywhere.
- Example: **Zoom** and **Slack** have become integral to team communication, while

Trello and **Asana** help you manage projects and tasks with ease, even when working with distributed teams.

B. Time Management and Productivity Apps

- Flexibility is all about making time work for you, not the other way around. Time management apps like **Notion**, **Todoist**, and **Google Calendar** help you organize your day, track progress, and stay focused.
- Studies show that **time management tools** can increase productivity by up to **25%** by reducing distractions and providing structure.
- Example: Use **Notion** to organize personal goals, work projects, and a daily to-do list all in one place, or set up automated reminders in **Google Calendar** to balance work commitments with personal priorities.

C. Financial Management for a Flexible Life

- Managing finances while living a flexible lifestyle can be challenging but is easily handled with the right tools. Apps like **Mint** and **YNAB (You Need a Budget)** track your spending, set savings goals, and help you stay on top of bills.

- **QuickBooks** and **Wave** are ideal for freelancers and entrepreneurs to manage invoices, track expenses, and even file taxes.
- Example: Sarah, a freelancer, uses **YNAB** to budget for irregular income and savings goals, ensuring she can travel without financial stress.

D. Health and Wellness Apps

- Flexibility doesn't just apply to work; your health and wellness routine must adapt, too. Apps like **Headspace** and **Calm** help you maintain mental clarity through meditation and mindfulness.
- Fitness apps like **Strava** and **MyFitnessPal** allow you to track workouts and nutrition, no matter where you are in the world.
- Example: After a long day of work, **Headspace** helps James unwind with guided meditation, while **Strava** keeps his daily exercise routine consistent, even while traveling.

E. Cloud Storage and Collaboration Tools

- With cloud-based tools like **Google Drive**, **Dropbox**, and **OneDrive**, your files are accessible from anywhere, allowing

seamless collaboration on documents and projects.
- These tools help ensure that even when you're on the move, you're not weighed down by the need to be in one place or dependent on physical devices.
- Example: Tina uses **Google Drive** to share presentations and reports with her team, making remote collaboration feel effortless.

Tips: Practical Strategies for Immediate Use

A. Embrace Automation

- Use tools like **Zapier** or **IFTTT** to automate repetitive tasks. For example, you can set up workflows to automatically save email attachments to your cloud storage or post your blog content to social media.
- Example: Automate client reminders or invoice generation, freeing up your time for more meaningful tasks.

B. Centralize Your Tasks and Projects

- Use **Notion** or **Trello** to keep everything in one place: work tasks, personal projects, and ideas. This reduces mental clutter and ensures nothing falls through the cracks.
- Example: Organize your week into work blocks and leisure time in **Notion**, and

prioritize each task according to importance and urgency.

C. Create a Flexible Work Setup

- Invest in portable, lightweight tech that allows you to work from anywhere—such as a reliable laptop, noise-canceling headphones, and a mobile hotspot for internet access.
- Example: Make use of coworking spaces and cafés when traveling. Apps like **WeWork** or **LiquidSpace** can help you find nearby workspaces with Wi-Fi.

D. Keep Communication Streamlined

- Use apps like **Slack** or **Microsoft Teams** to keep in touch with colleagues, while scheduling **Zoom** calls for face-to-face meetings.
- Example: Set up channels in **Slack** to discuss specific projects with your team or clients, ensuring communication remains organized and efficient.

E. Optimize for Remote Health

- Download wellness apps like **Headspace** for mental relaxation or **Strava** to track physical activity, ensuring you maintain

your health even when your routine is constantly shifting.
- Example: Block out time in your calendar for stretching or short walks during the day, and use an app like **MyFitnessPal** to stay on track with your fitness goals.

Analogies: Metaphors to Simplify Ideas

The Swiss Army Knife of Life

Think of your flexible lifestyle tools as a Swiss Army knife. Each app or technology serves a different purpose, from communication to time management, but when combined, they become powerful, helping you tackle various tasks with ease.

The Digital Backpack

Imagine carrying a lightweight backpack that holds everything you need: your work, your health routine, your finances, and your goals. Just like a backpack keeps your essentials organized and easily accessible, the right tools and apps keep your flexible life running smoothly, no matter where you are.

Summary: Key Takeaways and Next Chapter Preview

- **Key Takeaways**:

- The right tools and technologies empower a flexible lifestyle, allowing you to work, manage finances, and prioritize health from anywhere.
- Productivity apps, financial management tools, and wellness apps are essential for balancing your work and personal life.
- Cloud storage and collaboration tools ensure seamless communication and teamwork across different locations.

- **Next Chapter Preview**:
In the next chapter, we'll focus on building meaningful connections and networks that support your flexible lifestyle. Discover how cultivating relationships can expand your opportunities and enrich your journey.

CHAPTER 8: THE ART OF BALANCING HUSTLE AND HARMONY

Introduction: Hook and Chapter Purpose

In today's world, hustle culture often gets a bad rap, associated with burnout, stress, and an unhealthy obsession with constant productivity. But what if you could maintain the energy and ambition of the hustle without losing your sense of well-being?

In this chapter, we explore how to strike a balance between the relentless pursuit of your goals and the inner peace that comes with harmony. You'll learn how to navigate the delicate dance between pushing for success and taking the time to nurture yourself, your relationships, and your purpose.

Main Points: Explanation with Examples/Statistics

A. The Danger of the All-Consuming Hustle

- In a culture that glorifies non-stop work, many people push themselves to the point of exhaustion. According to a **Gallup study**, **23% of workers** experience burnout,

feeling that their work demands exceed their energy capacity.
- Example: Jack was working 60-hour weeks, convinced that his career would suffer if he slowed down. Eventually, he hit a wall, physically and mentally drained, realizing that his "hustle" wasn't sustainable in the long run.

B. The Need for Harmony and Recharge

- True success isn't just about what you achieve—it's about how you feel while achieving it. Mental health experts argue that taking breaks and having moments of stillness actually boost productivity and creativity.
- **Harvard Business Review** found that regular rest periods throughout the workday actually increase overall productivity by up to **20%**.
- Example: Lisa, a freelancer, found that after taking weekends off to recharge, she was more focused and energized during the workweek, completing projects faster and with higher quality.

C. The Synergy of Hustle and Harmony

- Achieving your goals requires drive and focus, but balancing that with self-care

creates a sustainable rhythm that promotes long-term success. Finding this balance doesn't mean sacrificing ambition; it means being intentional with how you allocate your energy.
- **Research from the National Institute of Health** shows that having a balanced approach to work-life integration can improve mental clarity, decrease stress, and lead to greater life satisfaction.
- Example: Sarah, an entrepreneur, balances long hours working on her startup with yoga, quality time with family, and personal hobbies. This balance fuels her creativity and passion, allowing her to work harder without burning out.

Tips: Practical Strategies for Immediate Use

A. Set Boundaries Around Work and Rest

- Define clear boundaries between work and downtime. Use tools like **time-blocking** to create specific times for work, family, hobbies, and relaxation.
- Example: Set specific hours during the day when you are available for work, and outside of those hours, disconnect completely.

B. Prioritize Self-Care as a Part of Your Hustle

- Just as you schedule meetings and deadlines, schedule self-care. This can include exercise, hobbies, meditation, or simply resting.
- Example: Block off time in your calendar for a daily walk, a weekend hobby, or an evening routine that allows you to recharge.

C. Embrace the Power of "Done is Better than Perfect"

- Striving for perfection can be paralyzing and counterproductive. Embrace progress over perfection, allowing yourself to complete tasks with confidence, even if they aren't flawless.
- Example: Focus on delivering a good product or service, rather than obsessing over every minor detail. You can always improve later, but first, prioritize completion.

D. Practice Mindful Hustling

- Be intentional with your actions. When you work, focus on the task at hand and give it your full attention. When you rest, fully engage in your downtime.

- Example: Try practicing **single-tasking** instead of multitasking to increase focus and reduce stress, whether you're working or relaxing.

E. Celebrate Small Wins

- Recognizing and celebrating your accomplishments, no matter how small, is a powerful way to maintain motivation while avoiding burnout.
- Example: After completing a challenging project, take time to reflect and reward yourself with something you enjoy, whether it's a small treat or a short getaway.

Analogies: Metaphors to Simplify Ideas

The Symphony of Life

Imagine your life as a symphony, where different instruments (work, rest, relationships, personal growth) come together to create harmony. If all the instruments played at full volume without pause, the music would be chaotic and exhausting. However, when they each take turns, adjusting to the rhythm, you get a balanced, beautiful melody that keeps you moving forward.

The Tug of War

Picture balancing hustle and harmony as a game of tug of war. On one side, you've got your hustle—the pull to achieve and accomplish. On the other side, there's harmony—the pull to rest and recharge. The key is not to let one side overpower the other, but to maintain a steady tension that keeps you moving forward without breaking the rope.

Summary: Key Takeaways and Next Chapter Preview

- **Key Takeaways**:
    - Hustle is necessary for success, but without balance, it can lead to burnout and fatigue.
    - Harmony is essential for maintaining mental clarity, creativity, and long-term productivity.
    - By setting boundaries, prioritizing self-care, and embracing progress over perfection, you can sustain both ambition and well-being.
- **Next Chapter Preview**:
    In the next chapter, we'll explore how to cultivate resilience in the face of challenges and setbacks. Discover the mindset shifts and strategies that will help you bounce

back stronger than ever, no matter what life throws your way.